volleyball

volleyball

BY
MARV DUNPHY

WITH
CARL GABLER

PHOTOGRAPHED BY
JOHN PARTIPILO

GROSSET & DUNLAP
A FILMWAYS COMPANY
Publishers • New York

Special thanks to the Pepperdine Varsity Teams for their participation in the photographic production of this book.

Contents

CHAPTER I

Introduction

The game of volleyball has become truly an international sport. The highest-ranking participant sport in the United States, volleyball appeals to players of all ages—at different levels of skill. Around the world, as many as 130 countries play the game, and it's estimated that 50 countries acknowledge this sport as a major one.

Volleyball was devised in 1895 by William G. Morgan, physical education director for the YMCA in Massachusetts. The game was originally called mintonette, until Professor Alfred T. Halstead of Springfield College renamed it. Although volleyball originated in the United States, it achieved its major sports status in Eastern Europe, where it became a highly competitive and skillfully played game. Until recently in the United States, it was mainly thought of as a recreational sport. That is changing. Amateur and collegiate teams are burgeoning, and professional leagues are expanding.

Still, for the weekend court or beach player, the game of volleyball remains a popular and accessible recreation. And its popularity is growing.

Now, in pictures, a beginning player can learn how to refine his techniques and get a better understanding of game strategy.

CHAPTER II

The Serve

In volleyball, the serve means much more than simply putting the ball into play. The server can send the ball to the opposing team in a way that will make it very difficult, if not impossible, to return the ball.

The three kinds of serves most commonly and effectively used will be shown: the underhand, the overhand floater, and the roundhouse. Because of the importance of the serve, it is necessary to master all three.

1 The Underhand Serve

2–1

This serve requires the least amount of skill and practice to perform. Because of its simplicity, beginning servers feel comfortable with it.

The serving hand (the right, if the player is right-handed) makes contact with the ball as shown in 2–1, with the heel of the hand and the knuckles of the little, ring, middle, and index fingers tucked in toward the palm. The thumb is tucked in toward the index finger.

A variation on this contact is shown in 2–2. The hand has now turned 90 degrees and the hitting platform is the flat surface made by the outer side of the index finger and the tucked-in thumb.

The body position for either of these hits is the same. The foot opposite the serving hand (in this, and in most cases, the left foot) is slightly in front of the right foot (2–3). The left—or tossing —hand holds the ball away from the body, with the left arm slightly bent at the elbow.

The serving arm moves back behind the right hip (2–4).

As the swing of the arm widens, the torso swivels from the hip toward the right (2–5).

When the serving arm has swung back to shoulder level (2–6), the left foot lifts and steps forward (2–7).

A full stride forward on the left foot is made as

2–2

2-3

2-4

2-5

2-6

2–7   2–8   2–9

the serving arm, held straight with a little bend at the elbow, swings toward the ball in the tossing hand (2–8).

At this point, the tossing hand slightly elevates the ball, then drops from under it. This movement is timed with the swing forward of the serving arm so that contact is made with the serving hand as the ball drops to waist level.

By 2–9, the ball is on its way. At the completion of this serve, the full weight of the body is on the left foot.

The torso and right leg now make a clean forward-leaning line (2–10).

In this sequence of pictures (2–3 to 2–10), the hitting platform of the serving hand has been made by the closed fist held with the index finger and tucked-in thumb aiming for the ball (as in 2–2).

In 2–11 through 2–15, the hitting platform is made with the closed fist—heel of the hand and knuckles of four fingers tucked toward the palm, all aiming at the ball (as in 2–1).

Incidentally, since the server in this series of pictures is left-handed, it's his right foot that steps forward and takes the weight of his body on the left-arm swing of his serve.

2–10

2–11

2–12

2–13

2–14

2–15

2 The Overhand Serve

The strategy of the overhand serve is to get the ball to "float" as it travels over the net. In this way, it's similar to the knuckleball in baseball, which is difficult for the batter to hit, just as the "overhead floater" can be a difficult serve to return.

Two elements are at work in causing this floating action. When the ball is contacted by the palm of the hand (stiff wrist), there is little or no wrist snap and no follow-through with the rest of the hand. This produces a flexing or distortion of the spheric shape of the ball. As it travels through space, it works to regain its original and natural shape: a perfect sphere. Its flight is marked by a kind of undulating movement, and so is easily affected by the changing air currents of the playing arena. By the time it reaches the other side of the net, a good floating ball can veer in either direction by as much as 4 or 5 feet. This makes the maneuver for a pass by the opponents a problem. It's important to remember that this floating action can be achieved only when there is no wrist snap and follow-through on contact with the ball. If there is, a spinning ball is the result, and a spinning ball will follow a true trajectory—precisely what is *not* wanted in an overhand floater.

The body position for the overhand floater is similar to that for the underhand. Again, the foot opposite the serving hand is slightly forward. The ball is held in the tossing hand, away from the body and in front of the serving hand shoulder, at about its level (2–16).

2–16

The toss begins in 2–17 and will go no higher than 3 or 4 feet above the head.

The serving arm, bent at the elbow, rises to shoulder level and is pulled back behind the head (2–18). Now the weight of the body is evenly distributed on both feet.

The serving arm is raised up from the shoulder line and the forearm is brought into play, preparing the serving hand for contact with the ball (2–19).

As the serving arm swings forward, the weight of the body is shifted to the opposite, forward foot, and the serving hand is held loosely at the wrist. On contact with the ball, the wrist stiffens and there is no follow-through. The contact is made above the head, as high as possible and always in front of the serving shoulder (2–20). Any crossover movement of the serving arm toward the opposite shoulder must be avoided.

2–17

2–18

2–19

2–20

3 The Roundhouse Serve

2–21

The roundhouse floater and the roundhouse spinner are both useful roundhouse serves.

The roundhouse floater is akin to the overhand floater in that the purpose of this serve is a veering action as it reaches the opponents' side. It likewise is achieved by a stiff-wrist, no-follow-through action of the serving hand on contact with the ball.

In the roundhouse spin, a true trajectory for the ball is the goal. With the proper amount of force and control behind this hit, a good topspin is produced for a truly effective serve.

2–21 shows the starting position for the roundhouse spin. No foot forward here.

The tossing hand and arm move up on a line with the tossing arm shoulder, while the serving arm, held straight with no bend at the elbow, moves back behind the hip (2–22).

The ball is tossed about 5 feet above the head and the leg opposite the serving arm bends slightly at the knee to accommodate a swiveling action at the hip toward the serving arm (2–23).

Now the serving arm is behind the back at waist level (2–24), and the tossing arm is still raised and pointing toward the ball in toss above the head.

When the ball has reached the top of its toss,

2–22   2–24

2–23

the serving arm swings forward as the tossing arm moves down (2-25), and the body weight now shifts to the foot opposite the serving arm.

The serving shoulder swivels forward so that both shoulders now face the net (2-26).

Contact with the ball starts with the heel of the hand, which then snaps at the wrist, bringing into play the palm and fingers of the hand that now contact the surface of the ball for the full force of the hit. This produces the essential and desired topspin.

By 2-27, the hit has been made and the weight of the body has now fallen completely on the foot opposite the serving hand.

The roundhouse floater requires the same body positionings as the roundhouse spin. The only thing different about it, as already suggested, is in the serving-hand contact with the ball.

The wrist remains stiff and contact with the ball is made only with the lower portion (heel) of the hand (2-28 to 2-31).

2-25

2-26

2-27

2–28

2–29

2–30

2–31

CHAPTER III

The Pass

The process of sending the ball to the setter on your team is known as the pass.

This is one of the most important skills to be learned in playing the game. The success of the offensive play depends largely on the initial pass on the service receive. Accuracy demands concentration, polished technique, and practice.

1 The Forearm Pass

3–1

3–1 shows the starting position or court position on the service receive pass. The legs are astride, with knees turned in toward each other (knock-kneed), and the arms rest at the side of the hips outside the knees. The weight of the body is forward, resting on the balls of the feet. In most cases, this forward body position is essential when making the pass.

3–2 shows the positioning of the arms and hands in preparation for the pass. The fingers are interlocked, the thumbs are forward, and the forearms are turned out. It is the flattened, turned-out forearms that will make the platform for the pass.

3–3 shows the full arm position with the elbows hyperextended and the entire length of the arm straight.

3–4 shows the hand-in-hand method. Here, the cupped left hand is placed inside the cushion of the right hand. Only the thumbs are joined in this position, and they are turned under.

Again, the elbows are hyperextended, the forearms turned out, and the length of the arm is held straight and away from the body (3–5). The forearm platform is now ready for the pass. No matter which hand grip is used, it must remain intact until the pass is made, and the forearm platform must remain away from the body.

3–2

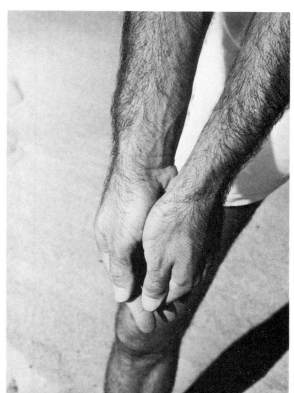

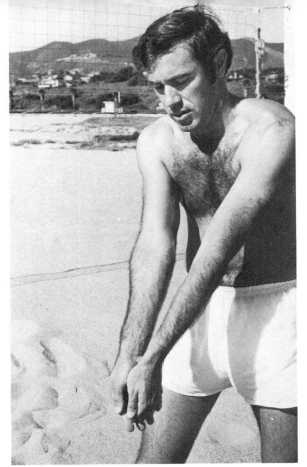

3–3

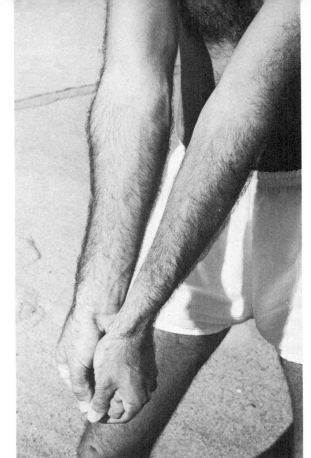

3–4

3–5

3–6

3–6 shows the contact with the ball on the pass. This should occur at a point somewhere above the bone structure of the wrist and on the rise of the forearm proper.

In the forearm pass (and in the overhand pass for the set, which will be discussed later), a common principle prevails: the passer's feet should not be in motion when making the pass. In addition, every effort should be made to pass the ball only when it reaches the midline (the vertical center of the body). This positioning will ensure an accurate aim on passing the ball. If the arms are away from this midline and at a lateral angle, the forearms will lose their level platform and the ball will likely hit only one arm and bounce off erratically.

A good way to avoid this lateral forearm angle is to "hop" or "skip" into position for the pass. Either one of these movements produces two desirable effects: (1) at the completion of the hop or skip, the player comes to a dead stop; (2) at the dead stop, the player is flexed into his body position and ready to place the weight of his body forward into the pass—almost to shovel the ball, instead of hitting it. This makes for a softer pass—almost always desirable.

In 3–7, the passer has initiated his hop, moving his left foot forward.

By 3–8, the player has completed the hop, come to a dead stop, and is moving forward into the ball with his body and passing platform.

3–9 shows the player raising his forearm platform to pass the ball.

In 3–10, the ball is seen shoveling off after the pass, with the player already pushing up on his back foot.

Notice in 3–8 to 3–11, the forearm platform is achieved by hyperextended elbows and straight arms held away from the body, while the player rises to meet and contact the ball on the midline.

3–7

3-8

3-9

3-10

3-11

3-11 shows the return of the player to an upright stance.

Concentration on the ball, so essential to a successful pass, begins with close observation of the server—if the ball is a service receive—or of the movement of the ball from player to player on the other side as it's in the process of being returned.

If the ball is being served, the passer should be aware of the direction the server has taken with his body position. Then quick observation should be made of the kind of contact the server has made with the ball (underhand, overhand, or roundhouse). The passer will then

have a fairly good idea where the ball will go, whether or not it's his or her ball to pass, and the movement he or she must make to execute that pass.

Pitfall to avoid in making the pass: a forearm platform that's not level. If one arm is slightly higher or lower than the other, the ball is likely to hit first one forearm and then the other, thereby producing a double hit and a violation. A forearm platform off the midline center should also be avoided, and the forearms should be held to produce a cushioned pass for the ball—not a swinging pass with force behind it. The cushioned pass, if properly aimed, will send the ball to its chosen destination.

2 The Lateral Pass

3-12

This is a last-resort technique for the pass, which, whenever possible, should be executed on the midline. With the lateral pass, the midline is ignored. If the player is not far enough behind the ball and it comes at him or her at a high angle, he or she must take it with a lateral pass away from the midline.

In 3-12, the left foot is forward in preparation for the pass.

In 3-13, the right foot steps forward and out to the side, as the left foot takes the body weight. The arms form their platform and begin their swing away from the midline and up to the right. The step to the side and the arm swing up is always taken in the direction the ball is coming—in this case, to the player's right.

As the step to the right is completed (3-14), the forearm platform rises to shoulder level on the right side and the body weight falls further back on the left leg, which bends at the knee.

As the ball comes in for the pass in 3-15, the player should make sure that his or her right arm is slightly higher than the left in making the final platform and swiveling the arms toward the floor. If the ball comes to the left and the platform is raised on that side, the left arm should be higher. If, as in this case, the right arm is in a slightly higher position, simultaneous contact with the ball and both arms is an almost automatic and desired result.

3-13

In 3–16, the player has pushed up on his right foot and swung his forearm platform against the ball for the pass, making sure he has chosen a trajectory for the ball. That trajectory is largely determined by the degree of the swing before contact with the ball is made on the pass.

3–15

3–14

3–16

CHAPTER IV

The Set

The passers move the ball to the setter at the net. This player, in turn, sets the ball up for a teammate, also at the net: the spiker.

Total control of the body and all its movements is critical in order to control the ball and its flight.

In the set, the ball must always be contacted at a point above and in front of the forehead and with all fingers of both hands simultaneously.

1 The Front Set

4–1

4–1 shows the basic hand position of the setter. The hands are open wide and far enough apart as if to accommodate the ball. The thumbs should be 1 to 3 inches apart, the index fingers 2 to 4 inches apart. (The distance will vary with individual hand size.) The thumbs form the base of a triangle, the index fingers its sides. The hands are held at forehead level, the upper arms at shoulder height. Contact with the ball will be made with the finger pads—not the fingertips.

4–2 shows the full body position, one foot in front of the other in preparation for body extension.

In 4–3, the hand and arm positions are seen from the side.

4–4 is a full side view of the body position. Notice that in this and the full front view of the body, the weight is forward—on the balls of the feet—as the setter moves into the set. As in the forearm pass, the set should not be executed while the player is in motion. Again, a preparatory hop or skip into position will be helpful to the player in positioning himself. This movement can be made to either side or forward. If the passer has sent the ball at a high angle, a hop or skip backward may be needed for the set.

From a side view, the player is raising his arms in 4–5. He has just completed his hop.

4–2

4-3

4-4

4-5

4-6

4-7

4-8

In 4-6, his hands are in position for the set and he is bending at the knees just before extending his body toward the ball.

Contact with the ball has been made in 4-7, all finger pads touching the ball at the same time. Arms and legs are extended in the upward movement of the extension. Follow-through with the arms and legs in this extending action is important. The hands alone cannot do the work. A mere stretching toward the ball and a mistaken contact with the fingertips is bad technique. The hands must always follow through in the direction the set is to take, never out at the sides (4-8).

4-9 to 4-11 show this sequence. Notice that in 4-12, at the top of the follow-through, the arms are fully extended and the feet have almost left the floor.

If the player executes a good set, it will almost seem as if he is holding onto the ball. The contact is soft and lifting. The wrists and forearms act as shock absorbers and help launch the ball. The wrists should be bent backward slightly to receive the ball. Upon contact with the ball, the wrists should bend back even further, then spring forward to make the launch. This wrist action works in conjunction with the arm and leg extension. Notice also that in 4-11 the elbows are held outside the shoulder line just prior to contact. In 4-12, they have straightened out with the arm's extension. This will prevent a drifting movement of the ball and ensure its trajectory to the spiker. The direction of that trajectory is determined by the positioning of the shoulders. They *must* face the direction the player wishes the ball to take. This is called "shoulder squaring."

4-9

4-10

4-11

4-12

Whenever possible, the setter should take the ball "overhand." Bump setting is another possible technique (it will be discussed later), but it's not preferred.

4–13 to 4–16 show a setter taking a low pass with an overhand. No time for a hop here.

In 4–14, his left leg slides out and his left foot pivots as it takes his body weight on the knee bend. The right leg is extended to the side and the arms are moving up to a setting position.

By 4–15, the player has fallen back to a sitting position in order to get behind the ball. The arms are extended for the contact and the hands are ready for the ball. The legs can't help here, so the arms do the work in launching the ball.

This has been done before the player completes his "cushion collapse" (4–16) with a full rollback. He will then roll to his side and push himself up to his feet as quickly as possible.

4–14

4–13

4–15

4–16

2 The Back Set

As in the front set, the aim here is to move the ball accurately to the spiker. The body and arm positions initiate as they do in the front set, but now, since the player's back is to the spiker, the arms in their extended position will follow the head, which will tilt back far enough to determine the ball's trajectory.

4–17 to 4–19 are almost identical to the front-set illustrations.

But by 4–20, the head has gone back and the arms are reaching over the head to contact the ball coming into frame at the top of the picture. The forward foot is taking the weight of the body.

Since the ball is to be sent to the spiker behind him, the player contacts the ball directly overhead and arches his back to launch it. The ball, in a sense, will be propelled backward—at least from the setter's point of view at that moment.

In 4–21, the ball has been launched and the player's arms follow through in the direction of the set.

Running too far under the ball is a common error made by the beginning player.

4–17

4–18

4–19

4–20

4–21

3 The Jump Set

This maneuver enhances the fast attack in volleyball. Body, arm, and hand positions are the same as in the front set, but now a jump is incorporated and it's initiated even before the arms are raised to front-set position (4–22).

In 4–23, the player is off the floor in his jump and the arms are being raised to make the contact.

Contact is made in 4–24. Since the player is off the floor, the legs cannot work to help launch the ball. Therefore the arms and wrists must do the job.

By 4–25, the ball has been contacted.

The jump set is most valuable in creating deception during the fast attack because it can look like a spike.

4–23

4–24   4–25

4–22

4 The Lateral Set

4–26

4–27

When the ball must be moved to the right or left and there is not time to face in the direction it will take, the lateral set comes into play.

Body and arm positions are the same as for the front set.

In 4–26, the player has thrown his weight on the right foot as the arms extend to make contact.

Contact and launch have been made in 4–27. Since the ball has been sent to the right, the left arm has reached higher than the right—*but* the contact was made with all fingers of both hands simultaneously.

The overextension of the left arm, seen clearly in 4–28, helps push the ball off to the right. The right arm is slightly bent to shorten its length. The torso leans toward the right.

The follow-through of this torso and arm extension to the right is seen in 4–29.

4–28

4–29

5 The Bump Set

This is essentially an underhand set and looks almost identical to the forearm pass—up to a point.

4–30 to 4–33 show typical body and arm positioning for the forearm pass.

But 4–34 reveals that the ball has not been shoveled. It has indeed been swung at with some force behind it. The forearm platform is up at shoulder level and the body is swiveling toward the spiker.

In 4–35, the spiker moves in to receive the ball.

The ball is spiked in 4–36.

4–30

4–31

4–32   4–33   4–34

4–35

4–36

CHAPTER V

The Spike

The spike is the key to successful offensive play, and the key to a successful spike is control of the body off the ground and full power behind the contact.

Three elements govern the spike: the approach, the jump, and the hit.

1 The Approach

5–1 shows the beginning of the approach toward the net.

In 5–2, the arms are dropping behind the hips in a backward swing.

The arms are fully extended behind the shoulders in 5–3. There are two reasons for this backswing of the arms: (1) their fast forward return will help pull the body up higher in its jump at the net; (2) the completion of this arm swing will bring the spiking arm into position for the hit.

5–2

5–1

5–3

2 The Jump

Both arms are coming up in front of the body as the jump at the net occurs in 5–4. The left arm acts as a guide. The right arm goes into position for the hit.

5–5 shows the right arm bending back at the elbow near the side of the head.

The player is at the top of his jump in 5–6, and the right arm is at "elbow high" or "elbow lead." It will now swing forward from the elbow to make contact with the ball above the right shoulder and on a direct line with it.

5–5

5–4

5–6

3 The Hit

When the ball is hit (5–7), the arm is fully extended. Contact has been made with the palm of the hand, with the wrist snapping freely. The power of the spike comes from a combination of arm speed and wrist snap—and somewhat from a flexing and rotating action of the upper body.

In 5–8 and 5–9 the player is dropping back to the ground and pulling his spiking arm in toward his body to avoid hitting the net.

5-7

5-9

4 Full Sequence

5-11

The spike is shown from the front in 5-10 to 5-17. And there is a difference: the spiker is on a hard ground surface, which gives him more momentum on his approach, and more height in his jump.

Once the hit is made in "elbow high" in 5-15, the left arm will drop to the side. The lateral pulldown of the left arm adds power to the right-arm hit. So does a flexing of the torso from the hips and a rotating action at the shoulders.

5-12

5-10

5-13

5-14

5-15

5-16

5-17

5 Line Spike

5-18 shows a player taking a spiker's angle hit and forcing the attacker to spike the line.

5-18

6 Angle Spike

In 5–19, the spiker has maneuvered around the block by hitting his spike at an angle and sending it across the court.

At no time does the spiker take his eyes off the ball to look at the block or another defensive player on the opposing team. Peripheral vision must suffice to tell the player whether or not he has a problem with the blocker and where he should hit the ball. This technique takes experience. Beginning players shouldn't expect it to come easily.

5–19

7 The Dink

Here it is in 5–20. The elements of approach and jump are the same as in the spike, but the hit is different. At the very last moment of contact, the ball is tipped with a stiff wrist. It is not hit with force. The wrist is not turned to aim the ball. It must face the direction the ball is to take. Clearly, the purpose of the dink is to deceive. The block on the other side of the net is expecting a spike and plays toward meeting it. He or she is not prepared for the soft drop of the ball in the dink.

5–20

8 Deep Court Spike

In 5–21, 5–22, and 5–23, the player is spiking the ball from about the 15-foot line. Generally in volleyball, only the front-row players can attack or spike at the net. But behind the 10-foot line, any one of the players can use the spike. The back-row players *must* spike from behind the 10-foot line. Only in a takeoff from behind the line can they travel over it.

The deep court spike differs from the spike at the net in that the player does not drive the ball toward a downward hit. The player will reach higher for the hit, have more wrist snap at the contact, and send the ball straight over the net into a deep corner of the court on the other side.

As can be seen in 5–21, the hitting arm is fully extended before the hit and the wrist is bent far back for a full snap.

5–22 shows more of the wrist action as the ball is launched.

In 5–23, the follow-through on the deep wrist snap is complete.

The deep court spike is given special mention because all players should be prepared to execute the spike, no matter what position they are playing. Most players are able to spike the ball on a good set, but the valuable player is able to spike on the bad set, the trouble set, and the deep set. Practice in getting a hit on these off-plays can only work to improve your game.

5–21

5–22

5–23

CHAPTER VI

The Block

Blocking is a difficult skill to learn. The technique is a combination of various elements, and each one must be studied and practiced separately. Then they must all be combined and executed at peak performance.

1 The Starting Position

6–1

When his or her team is serving, the blocker's starting position is about a good arm's length from the net (6–1). This will give the player room to take advantage of a service receive error by the opponent, who literally may set the ball up for the blocker to spike back. If the blocker is too close to the net, there won't be room to make the spike.

6–2 tells us that the pass on the other side has been good. The blocker will then step forward and "read" the opponents' offensive strategy.

In 6–3, he is taking the blocker's position at the net: hands are high, palms facing out; knees are slightly bent for the blocking jump.

Though the blocker follows the progress of the ball on the other side from passer to setter, his main concern will be the hitter. The angle taken by the hitter's hips will tell the blocker something about the direction the spike will take. A drop of the hitter's shoulder may indicate the direction of the spike. The hitter's eyes tell a story, too, for they are spotting a target for the ball. The blocker can make a judgment on that visual fix.

6–2

6–3

2 The Blocking Jump

6–4 shows the standard blocking jump. The arms are held high, extended; the hands are open, with palms toward the net. The hands are no more than a foot apart. The hands have penetrated the vertical line above the net. They may reach across this line to intercept or block the ball. They may not reach over to spike the ball before it has traveled over the net.

Very important: The blocker must always execute his jump *after* the spiker has jumped. The spiker has the greater momentum from his approach. The blocker must jump from in place. If the blocker's jump is properly timed, he will reach the spiker's height for contact with the ball and so be in a position for an effective block. If the blocker makes the mistake of jumping with the spiker, he'll be dropping back down at the moment the spiker has reached the top of his jump and is making contact with the ball.

6–4

3 The Outside Blockers

These are the two players on the front line at either side of the court. Their job is to set the block, line up on the hitter, and then work with the middle blocker to take the spike.

The outside blocker will keep his outside arm turned somewhat inward to prevent the spiker from hitting that arm with the ball, thereby deflecting it out of bounds.

In 6–4 again, the player is placing his right arm slightly forward (since he is on the right side of the court, this is his outside arm). This should avoid a deflecting hit on that arm.

6–5 shows a common blocking technique: a jump straight up to take the hitter's line.

Then in 6–6, a quick lateral move of the arms to the right (or left) picks up on the hitter's obligatory change of line.

6–7 shows this maneuver with the hitter.

In 6–8, the middle blocker has joined the outside blocker for a two-man block. The outside blocker faces the hitter head on with his right arm turned inward. The middle blocker's presence on his partner's left cancels out the spiker's alternative for a hit away from the outside blocker.

6–5

6–6

6–7

6–8

4 The Middle Blocker

6-9

In 6–9 to 6–13, the middle blocker's basic maneuver is shown: joining the outside blocker for a two-man block.

The slide step to the right (or left) begins in 6–9.

The player continues his slide step in 6–10.

In 6–11, he has completed his right-foot slide.

He pulls his left foot over in 6–12 and is easily in position for the two-man block.

The jump by both players (6–13) is simultaneous. If there is any space gap between these two players, it is the responsibility of the outside blocker to close it up.

Another maneuver for reaching the outside blocker is shown in 6–14 to 6–17. This is the crossover step. The center blocker, realizing the set has gone to the outside, will turn and run to meet the outside blocker.

In 6–14, he begins his turn.

He has crossed over—not in a slide to the side but with a deliberate quick-stepping movement (6–15).

By 6–16, he is at the outside blocker's side, feet planted firmly, his blocking arms raised and hands facing the net.

6-10

6–11

6–12

6–17 shows the simultaneous jump to block the spike.

6–18 shows the two blockers in concert at the top of their jump. Once they have intercepted the ball and it has gone by them, their job is to keep an eye on it, turning with it as it travels on behind them.

6–19 shows this turning of the head as the blockers drop down from their jump.

By 6–20, they are on the ground and are already turning to the left to follow the ball's trajectory to their own passers.

In 6–21, they are coming off the net in preparation for the spike. Getting away from the net is essential at this point. It can be very discouraging for the setter if his blockers are not in position to take his set for a spike.

The middle blocking position is clearly a crucial one, since it not only blocks from the center but goes to either side for a two-man block.

6–13

6-14

6-15

6-16

6-17

6-18

6-19

6-20

6-21

CHAPTER VII

Individual Defense

What follows are the individual defensive tactics that can be employed by the player. Here, there are five elements to explore: the starting position, the arm dig (or power dig), the roll, the overhead dig, and the dive.

1 The Starting Position

7-1 shows the starting or court position. The body is in a fairly low crouch, with the knees bent and turned inward (knock-kneed) between the toes—as in the stance for the forearm pass. Here the feet are turned slightly out, and they are placed outside the shoulder line. The arms—with a slight bend at the elbow—are held down at the sides with cupped hands (palms facing inward), level with the knees. The body weight is on the balls of the feet and is thrown slightly forward. This position should be played to accommodate a move *forward* toward the approaching ball.

7-1

2 The Arm Dig

7–3

7–2 through 7–5 show the sequence for the standard two-arm dig—sometimes called a power dig. The two-arm dig offers better control, and thus is the preferred maneuver.

The starting position is shown in 7–2. The player has come out of his crouch to meet the approaching ball.

In 7–3, the arms have come together as in the forearm pass. The knees are moving inward for support.

7–4 shows a drop in body position in preparation to cushion the ball—on the midline at all times.

In 7–5, the player's shoulders shrug to pull the arms into position for a cushion contact with the ball, thus absorbing its speed.

7–4

7–2

7–5

3 The Roll

7–6

7–7

7–8

The roll and the dive are defensive tactics of last resort. The aim here is to play the ball coming in at an oblique angle.

In 7–6, the player starts with a low, crouching step toward the incoming ball at the right—a step made off to the side. Her right arm begins its extension to dig the ball.

The player has contacted the ball with a one-arm dig in 7–7, and she is already pivoting on her right foot, which is taking the body weight. By the time the foot is pivoting, the player is sitting on the floor.

In 7–8, the digging arm has gone to the floor and is used as a lever to propel the player into a leftward rolling motion on her back. She then pushes even further up toward the left shoulder.

7–9 shows the right arm extended to support the left shoulder roll, as well as a throwing of the legs overhead and back down toward the floor.

The player recovers in 7–10 and pushes up with both arms.

By 7–11, her arms have come forward again in preparation for another dig.

7–12 brings her back to a starting position.

7–13 through 7–19 show the same lateral roll, but this time with a two-arm dig.

7–9

7–10

7–11

7–12

This time, with both arms up in the air after the dig (7-16), she will start the roll on her buttocks before falling onto her back (7-17).

Since the dig has been made on the right, the roll will be executed to the left with completion over the left shoulder and recovery made with leverage from both arms bent under the body (7-18).

Pushing up with the hands in 7-19 gets the player back into starting position.

7-14

7-13

7-15

7–16

7–17

7–18

7–19

4 The Overhead Dig

When the ball comes in at a high angle and the forearm dig won't work, the overhead is used. This is a legal maneuver provided the ball in no way rests on the turned-in forearms but bounces off in a clean hit.

7-20 and 7-21 show this hit.

7-20

7-21

5 The Dive

7-22

7-22 through 7-27 break down, step by step, the body positionings during the dive.

In 7-22, the player is in a starting position for a teaching progression on the dive.

In 7-23, the player lowers his torso to the floor.

By 7-24, the player has begun his belly slide.

Chest and upper legs are now in full contact with the floor (7-25), and the hands are acting as levers to slide the body forward.

The slide is completed with the back fully arched, the chin up, the head forward, the knees off the floor, and the arms back at the sides (7-26).

7-27 shows a different starting position for the same teaching progression. The player has catapulted himself into a dive. Now he will follow through with the body positionings of 7-23 through 7-26.

Another teaching progression—using the ball—is begun in 7-28.

The ball is rolled by the coach to the player in 7-29.

The dig is made by the player in 7-30.

In 7-31, the player has dived (as in 7-27).

The belly slide is seen in 7-32. It is crucial to

7-23

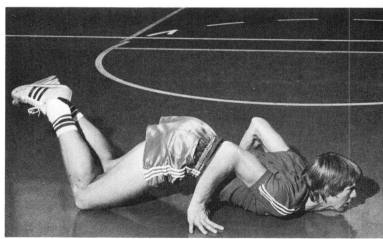

7-24

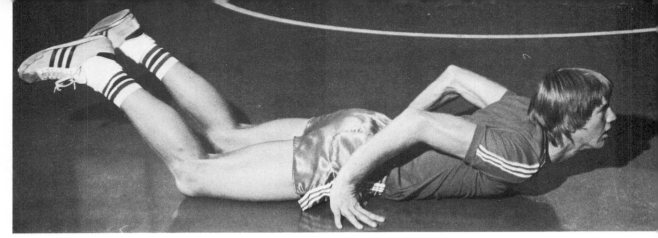

7-25

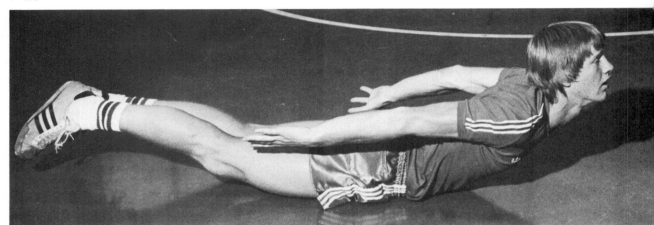

7-26

7-27

get the hips squared with the floor and the legs off the floor.

By 7–33, the player has pulled through his slide and is about to recover.

7–34 through 7–36 show a front view of a fully extended midair dive.

Notice that after the hit in 7–34, one leg is already up behind the player and the push-off leg, still on the floor, will serve to propel the player forward.

In 7–35, both legs are up in the air behind the player and the arms are fully extended.

7–28

7–29

7–30

7–31

7–36 shows the arms moving down to the floor to support the dive and the beginning of the belly slide. The legs are high in the air, not dragging.

7–37 through 7–46 show the dive incorporated with the backhand dig.

7–37 shows the beginning of a run toward the ball, with the arms swinging back behind the hips (7–38).

By 7–39, the chest is lowering in preparation for the dive. Notice the eye contact with the ball.

The forward foot is driving off for the catapult into the dive (7–40).

In 7–41, the right arm is moving forward to hit the ball with the back of the hand, snapping the back of the wrist and arm.

By 7–42, the dig has been made and both feet are in the air.

7–32

7–33

7–34

7–35

7–36

7–37

7–38

7–39

7–40

7–41

7–42

The arms come toward the floor in 7–43.

The hands make contact with the floor on the dive in 7–44.

7–45 shows the start of the belly slide.

And finally, the follow-through is seen in 7–46.

7–43

7–44

7–45

7–46

CHAPTER VIII

Offensive Team Play

There are two basic offensive strategies: the two-hitter attack and the three-hitter attack.

The two-hitter attack applies in the 4-2 system. In the 4-2 system, one of the three front-row players functions primarily as a setter, while the other two play as hitters. The advantages of this system are its simplicity and the security of having a setter on the front line. Very few errors are made with this system, and it should be used by most beginning players.

In the 6-2 system, a player from the back row comes up to set the ball and all three front-row players are hitters. Highly skilled players prefer the 6-2 since it allows for three attackers on the front line.

1 The 4-2 System

8–1

8–1 shows a 4-2 system with the setter positioned at right-front. The setter lines up close to the net and the hitter in the middle position moves to the right to take the ball from the setter, who will move in toward center.

The setter is in the center-front position in 8–2, his starting position for the service receive. Notice that this alignment of team players (back and front row) forms a letter W or M, depending on whether it is seen from the rear or the front. The W or M formation is the basic alignment of players for a service receive, giving the team its best court coverage.

In 8–3, the setter is in the left-front. The middle hitter will move toward the outside as the setter moves in to meet him just off-center for the set and spike.

See DIAGRAM A for a complete look at the 4-2 system.

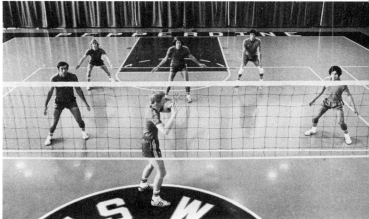

8–2

8–3

OFFENSE
4-2 Service Reception

A.

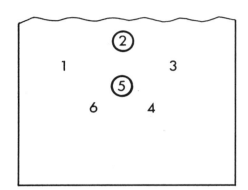

1. Numbers 2 and 5 are the setters, and are always opposite each other.

2. 3 and 6 are the best attackers, and will hit twice from the left side of the court.

3. Serve reception is a basic W formation.

B.

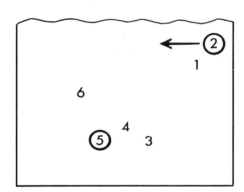

1. As soon as the server contacts the ball, 2 moves to the center of the net to receive the pass.

2. The setter should face the best attacker and set him whenever possible.

C.

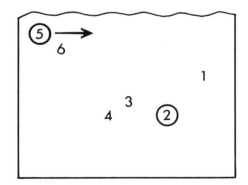

1. As soon as the server contacts the ball, 5 moves to the center of the net and turns to face the strongest hitter.

COMMENTS:

1. This is a simple system and easy for players.

2. This system is especially effective if the team has only two strong hitters.

3. This system is less effective when the opposition has strong blockers.

4. This system is good with beginning players.

2 The 6-2 System

8–4

8–5

8–6

In 8–4, the three front-row hitters are positioned just behind the 10-foot line. The back-row players line up behind the holes in the front line. The third back-row player in the right-back corner of the court is the setter. Immediately after the opposing side has served the ball, he moves to the right-center of the net. He will face the middle hitter and the left-front hitter. They are his on-hand hitters (if they are right-handed). The third hitter in the right-front court is the off-hand hitter (if he is right-handed).

The setter is in the center-back position in 8–5, and will line himself up behind the center-front hitter on a line with that player's right hip. After contact on the serve, the setter will move in toward the right-center of the net to set the ball.

The setter is now in the left-back (8–6) and will again move up to the right-center at the net on the contact of the serve.

The 6-2 offense usually demands a fast attack from the center hitter, who more often than not jumps to spike even before the setter has set the ball. He thereby creates a deception for the opposing blockers, drawing them away from his own outside hitters.

In both systems, all players must be prepared to play the ball in the event that the spiker's hit is blocked and the ball comes back into the court. The ball should then be passed high by the recovering player to allow time for the setter to move in for another set and then a spike. This "all-team alert" is called hitter coverage.

See DIAGRAM B for a complete look at the 6-2 system.

Diagram B

OFFENSE
6-2 Reception

A.

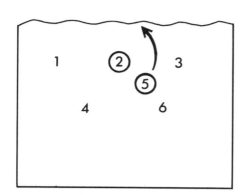

1. 1, 2, and 3 are front-row hitters.

2. As soon as the server contacts the ball, 5 moves to right-center of net.

3. All three front-row hitters are eligible to attack the ball.

4. 2 will hit a short set at the center of the net.

B.

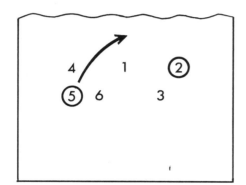

1. As soon as the server contacts the ball, 5 moves to right-center and faces 1 and 4.

2. Serve reception is the same W pattern.

C.

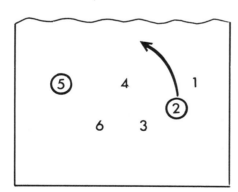

1. As soon as the server contacts the ball, 2 moves to right-center.

D.

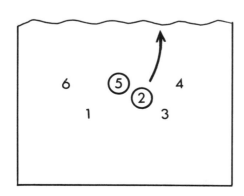

COMMENTS:

1. This offense is effective only if the team is a good passing team.

2. The strategy of this offense is to force the opposing middle blocker to stay in the middle.

3. The idea is to create a one-on-one, or maybe a one-on-none, hitting situation.

CHAPTER IX

Defensive Team Play

There are three types of defenses played: the red, the white, and the blue. The most commonly used is the white, also referred to as the "man back defense."

1 The Red

The red defense involves bringing a player from the back row to a position on the 10-foot line behind the block. In 9–1, this player is seen just behind the blockers in the down-right area of the court. He must cover behind the block in the event of a dink or off-speed shot just off the block. The two players remaining in the back row are responsible only for a dig on a driven ball. The red defense can be effectively used against a team that dinks and tips the ball frequently, or a team that doesn't have effective spikers.

9–1

2 The White

9–2 shows the white defense. Here, all three back-row players stay in the back row. The left-front blocker moves slightly away from the net, remaining inside the 10-foot line. The dink is covered by the right-back player and the off-blocker. Experienced teams will use the white defense.

9–2

3 The Blue

This defense is shown in 9–3. This maneuver brings the off-blocker (left-front) over behind the block to cover for the tip or off-speed shot over the block. Again, the three back-row players are concerned only with digging the driven ball. The one disadvantage of this defense is that the off-blocker, who is covering behind the block, has little time to get back into spiking position on the left-front. If the ball gets over the block and is set up to this player by a team member, he must be ready to receive it for the spike.

9–3

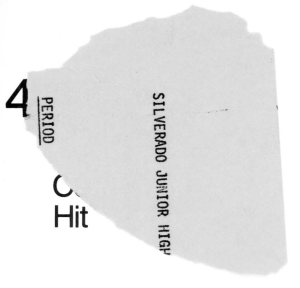

4 PERIOD

Center
Hit

As seen in 9–4, the middle blocker has the
initial responsibility for stopping the center hit.
The left back and right back (wing diggers)
should be ready to dig this quick hit if it gets by
the middle blocker.

9–4

CHAPTER X

Recreational Play

The sequence in 10–1, 10–2, and 10–3 shows coeducational team play with three men and three women on each side. In coeducational team play, a rule dictates that when more than one contact with the ball is made on one side, one of those contacts must be made by a woman player. And if there is only one male player in the front line, he can be joined by another male player from the back row to help block, but this back-row player may not hit the ball.

Informal recreational play seldom adheres to these special coed rules, but in YMCA or Community Center games, such rules are often strictly enforced.

Mixed-doubles team play is shown in 10–4 and 10–5. Here it's boy-girl against boy-girl—two players on each side. In beach play with this team lineup, players are not allowed to block over the net. The net is slightly lower than in standard play—about 7 feet, 10 inches high as opposed to 8 feet.

10–1

10–4

10–2

10–5

10–3

CHAPTER XI

Warmups

Essential to competition players, and recommended for recreational players, are warmups to get ready for the game. The stretching exercises are a must for all players—they are the best way to avoid strains and sprains. Here are several warmup techniques. Find the one or two that suit your needs and spend a little time on them before starting your game.

11–1

11–2

11–3

11–4

11–1 shows a simple jog. This gets the vascular system going. A one- to two-minute light jog can start you off.

11–2 shows the lateral jog—a simple step to the side and a closing-up step with the other foot. The follow-up foot does not cross over.

An about-face and a continuous sidestepping jog are shown in 11–3.

A backward jog (11–4).

11–5

11–6

11–7   11–8

11–5 is the crossover jog step.

A circle jog (11–6).

11–7: the elephant walk—or a long stride with each step and an arm swing out to the side.

The elephant walk again (11–8) but now the arms swing up and down.

11–9 shows the wrestler's hold. You clearly need a partner for this one. Standing about 5 feet apart, facing each other, interlock arms and bend from the waist to form a bridge. Your hands should stay on your partner's shoulders.

A turnout to one side from the hip (11–10) involves torso only; legs and feet don't move.

A reverse swing to the other side (11–11).

11-9

11-10

11-11

11–12 shows the lateral stretch. Stand side by side with your partner. Brace your foot against his. Your outside arm goes over your head to grasp his hand on his outside arm. The inside hands are held. The outside legs move to the side. Now pull gently to the outside. Reverse positions to stretch out those side muscles. These stretches are held for a count of two.

Picture sequence 11–13 through 11–15 shows a back and shoulder stretch. Knees are on the floor, arms go forward, head stays down. First with both arms, then the right with the head turned toward the left, then the left with the head turned toward the right.

The truck twist is shown in 11–16 and 11–17. Be sure your shoulders remain flat on the floor. The toe touch to the hand should be held for two counts.

The legover is shown in 11–18. A good stretch for the lower back.

11–12

11–13

11–14

11–15

11-16

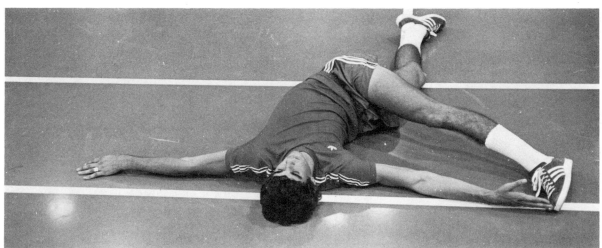

11-17

11-18

11–19

A hamstring stretch is shown in 11–19. The right knee is brought up to the left shoulder against the chest, and it should stay there for a slow count of four. Alternate with left knee to right shoulder. Do not raise the shoulder to meet the knee.

Side and front views of a simple back arch in 11–20 and 11–21. This exercise is a must for a player skillful enough to execute the dive. Lifting the head high and looking up will produce the stretch in this one.

The upper leg muscles get it in 11–22 and 11–23. Again, the head is held high and the thighs are pulled off the floor.

11–20

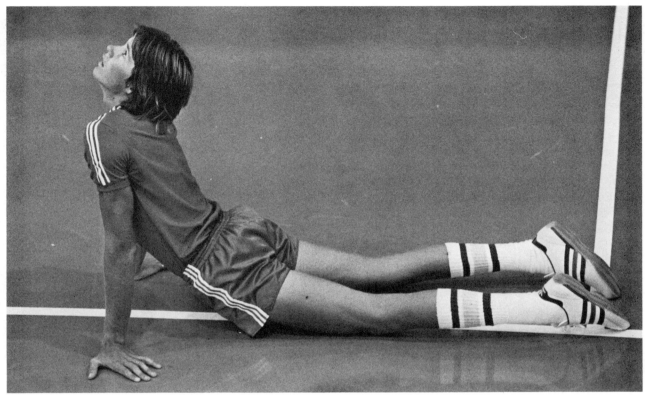

11–21

11–22

11–23

CHAPTER XII

Basic Rules and Regulations

Scoring.   Games are played to 15 points. The game must be won by a margin of 2 points. Only the serving side can make a point. When the opposing side completes a spike against the serving side, or when the serving side sends a ball out of bounds, the opposing side does not score. It merely gains the serve. This is a "side out."

Matches.   Best three out of five games wins. Or two out of three games in a short match.

Rotations.   Players rotate clockwise toward the serving position on every side out.

Time outs.   Two per game are allowed.

Substitutions.   U.S. rules say two per game. International rules permit six. Substitutes are allowed to reenter the game twice in the United States. International rules do not permit reentry.

Serve.   (1) You may not step on or over the end line until the ball is served. (2) You must serve within the 10-foot serving area. Depth of the serve is infinite.

Contacts.   International rules limit ball contact to three hits on one side before the ball is passed over the net; four, if one of the three is the result of a block.

The Pass.   (1) The ball must be contacted with both arms simultaneously. A double contact is a violation. (2) The pass cannot be made with open hands.

The Set Overhead Pass.   (1) Simultaneous contact with all fingers of both hands. If not, a double hit or throw is called. (2) The ball may have momentary rest during the recoiling action, but it may not be held—a violation.

The Block.   (1) Player may reach over the net when blocking. (2) Serve cannot be blocked or spiked with a reach over the net. (3) No part of the body is allowed to touch the net. (4) Only front-row players may block. (5) The blocker may play the ball a second time if the ball is hit off him during the blocking attempt. (6) Blockers on the serving side cannot form a screen for the server.

The Spike.   (1) Spikers cannot reach over the net to spike the ball. Spikers are allowed to follow through over the net if the initial contact has been made on their side of the net. (2) All players are allowed to spike from behind the 10-foot line. Only front-row players may spike when inside the 10-foot line. (3) The ball must be clearly hit when spiking with an open hand. Guiding or carrying the ball is a violation unless it's done with fingertips and a stiff wrist, as in the tip or the dink.

Violations. When a violation is called, the side penalized will lose service or a point will go to the opposing side.

See Diagram C for volleyball court dimensions.

Diagram C

VOLLEYBALL COURT AND DIMENSIONS

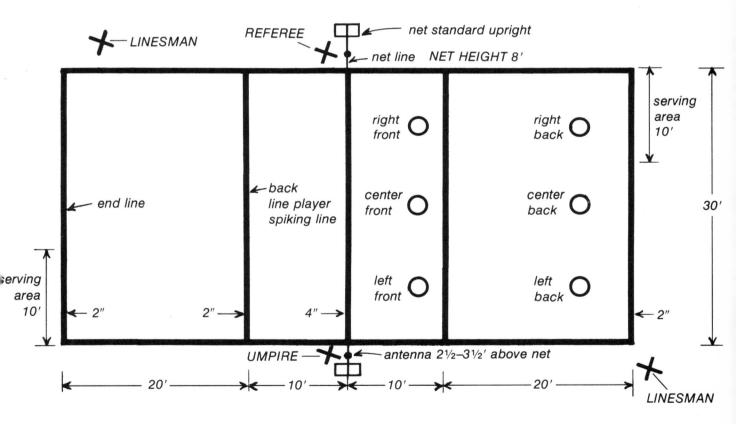

CHAPTER XIII

Amateur and Professional Competition

The United States Volleyball Association (USVBA) was established in 1928. This organization is directly affiliated with the United States Olympic Committee and is the main governing body for volleyball throughout the country.

The USVBA coordinates regional tournament play. There are 19 regions, and each is autonomous. The season is from November to May, and there is a playoff for National Championship. Team categories are: Men, Women, Masters (35+), and Collegiate.

The National Collegiate Athletic Association supervises national championship intercollegiate volleyball for men. The varsity season is from February to April.

The Association for International Athletics for Women supervises national championship intercollegiate volleyball for women. The varsity season is from September to December.

Pro volleyball has two leagues: Eastern and Western. Teams are coeducational: two women, four men. The season is from June to August.

The USVBA and the U.S. Olympic Committee send teams, which they have put together from amateur and collegiate groups, abroad on tours—to the World Games, Pan-American Games, and the Olympics. For the American team to qualify for the Olympics, it must place first in competition among all teams from Central and North America.

Glossary

Cushion—taking the speed off the ball.

Dink—(tip) ball tipped with stiff wrist for soft drop.

Float—a veering action of the ball in the floater serve.

Follow-through—completed motion.

Line—side boundary line.

Midline—vertical center of the body.

Off-hand—set coming from the left for a right-handed person.

Off-speed—soft spike.

On-hand—set coming from the right for a right-handed person.

Platform—contact surface for the ball.

Shovel—forearm motion in the pass.

Topspin—fast spinning action of the ball.

About Marv Dunphy

Born and raised in Topanga Canyon, California, Marv Dunphy is a graduate of Pepperdine University with a BS degree in Kinesiology. Mr. Dunphy was a standout player of the Pepperdine Varsity team and then became its head coach. In 1975, he was assistant coach for the U.S. team at the Pan-American Games in Mexico City. In 1976, he was assistant coach for the U.S. team at the Olympic Qualifying Tournament in Rome, Italy. In that same year, he was head coach for the U.S. team in its match with Japan and The People's Republic of China. Also in 1976, he was appointed head coach by the USVBA for their Olympic Development Camp at Santa Barbara, California.

Index